Concert Etude

ALEXANDER GOEDICKE
Op. 49

Alexander Goedicke

CONCERT ETUDE

Opus 49

for Bb Trumpet (Cornet) and Piano

Concert Etude

Op. 49

By ALEXANDER GOEDICKE

Alexander Fyodorovich Goedicke is one of the older of the contemporary composers in the Soviet Union, having been born in Moscow on March 2, 1877. His has been a career full of prestige and honors. As a teacher he has always been held in high regard; in his role of professor at the Moscow Conservatory, he has influenced generations of musicians and composers. As a composer, he began to win honors as early as 1900 when he captured the Rubinstein Prize for Composition. Since then he has produced compositions in all categories in a prolific flow.

Of particular interest to us are the works he has written for solo wood-wind and brass instruments. Among these we find a *Concerto for French Horn*, a *Concerto for Trumpet* and the one under present consideration, a *Concert Etude for Trumpet*. This was originally written for trumpet and orchestra but is here presented with a piano accompaniment reduced from the original score by the composer.

The *Concert Etude* is written along fairly "classical lines", which is not too difficult to understand since Goedicke is one of the greatest living exponents of the "Western Tradition" in Russia. The word "Etude" which ordinarily connotes a dry-as-dust study is qualified with the word "Concert" by the composer. It follows along the lines of the Chopin *Etudes* for piano which have always been used both as study and concert material. The opening theme has the light, airy character of a Mozart *Rondo* or Mendelssohn *Scherzo*. The secondary theme, which appears at [5], is in direct contrast and has broad, flowing lines. The tonguings should all be soft and the player should take short breaths so that all the notes will appear connected.

ALEXANDER GOEDICKE

CONCERT ETUDE
OPUS 49

FOR Bb TRUMPET (CORNET) AND PIANO

Concert Etude

Trumpet in Bb

ALEXANDER GOEDICKE
Op. 49

Allegro molto

Trumpet in Bb

Trumpet in Bb

HAL•LEONARD® CORPORATION

7777 W. BLUEMOUND RD. P.O. BOX 13819 MILWAUKEE, WI 53213

0-73999-28790-5

HL00121835

U.S. $9.99

ISBN 978-0-634-06145-5